How to Be a Good Baseball Player

tips on batting, pitching, fielding

by Clare and Frank Gault

Illustrated by Dick Ericson

SCHOLASTIC INC.
New York Toronto London Auckland Sydney

To Marsha, Bryan, and Dave,
who have kept us involved
in sports for years

ISBN 0-590-05010-9

21 20 19 18 17 16 15 14 13 12 11   6 7 8 9/8 0/9

Printed in the U.S.A.   07

tips on batting

Picking the best bat for you

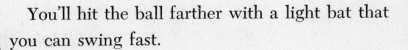

The best bat for you will be the most comfortable to swing. So pick one that feels light.

You'll hit the ball farther with a light bat that you can swing fast.

You'll swing a heavy bat more slowly and won't hit the ball as far.

Also, a light bat is easier to control while you're swinging. So you'll be able to hit the ball more often.

How can you tell if a bat is light enough?

Pick one up and hold it the way you would if you were at bat. Is it easy to hold off your shoulder?

Now, swing it a couple of times. Can you swing it fast?

When you swing it, do you feel you have complete control of it?

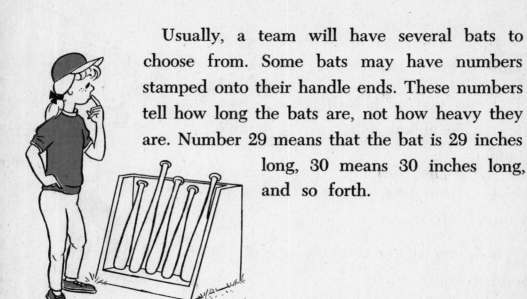

Usually, a team will have several bats to choose from. Some bats may have numbers stamped onto their handle ends. These numbers tell how long the bats are, not how heavy they are. Number 29 means that the bat is 29 inches long, 30 means 30 inches long, and so forth.

Often, the shorter bats are lighter, but not always. Try them all, and pick one that feels light.

If you've tried them all and still wish you could have a lighter one, use one of the longer bats and "choke up" on it. Grip the bat a few inches up on the bat handle. This will make the bat "feel" lighter and you'll be able to swing it better.

Standing at the plate—batting stances

You're you. There's no one exactly like you. So you'll have to find out for yourself which is the best way for you to stand at the plate. Often, the best way is the most comfortable, the way that feels most natural to you.

There's no use trying to copy someone else. Everybody is built differently. That's why you see so many different batting stances.

A good place to start in finding your own batting stance is with the "normal" hitting position.

13

Stand with your toes a few inches from the plate.

Spread your feet enough to give you a good steady feeling. But keep them close enough together so that you can shift from one foot to the other easily.

Bend your body just a bit toward the plate and hold your bat up off your shoulder.

Now you're in good position to see the pitch and ready to take a full swing. When you find a way that feels better and that works—use it.

Getting base hits

It's not easy to hit a baseball. It takes plenty of practice. No player expects to get a base hit every time, or even most of the time. Even the best hitters in the big leagues get a base hit only about once for every three official times at bat.

But *feel* lucky. It helps, You'll get more base hits if you think you're going to hit every time. You'll swing the bat better and stronger.

Where you swing your bat, of course, is very important. You want to hit the ball where it's hardest for the fielders to get.

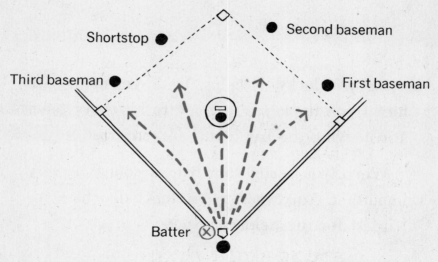

Shortstop

Second baseman

Third baseman

First baseman

Batter

Suppose you swing and hit a ground ball. If you hit it fast enough and where a fielder isn't, you'll probably get a base hit.

But there are four infielders plus the pitcher and catcher, so it's hard to hit a ground ball through the infield. The odds are against it.

Suppose you bat under the ball and hit a high fly. Now a fielder has a chance to move under it and make the catch—unless it's over the fence for a homer. There are very few homers, but plenty of high flies are caught for outs. A high fly doesn't have much chance to be a real hit.

What's left? Low fly balls and line drives. They're almost the same. Both are hit into the air but not too far off the ground. A line drive is just hit faster and harder than a low fly

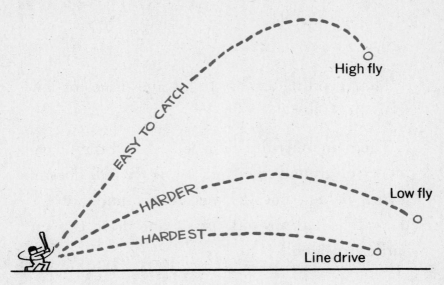

EASY TO CATCH

High fly

HARDER

Low fly

HARDEST

Line drive

21

Most good batters try to hit line drives or low fly balls. Why?

There are only three outfielders and they have plenty of ground to cover. A low fly ball doesn't give a fielder much chance to get under it for the catch. It drops too fast. A line drive is even harder to catch.

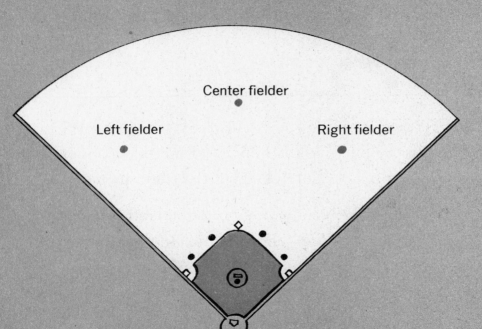

Center fielder

Left fielder

Right fielder

23

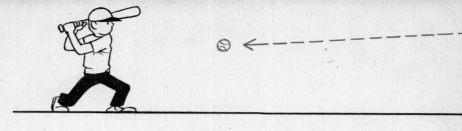

How do you hit line drives? By swinging level with the pitch, in the same path the pitch comes to the plate. Let's think about that for a moment.

The pitcher is standing on the mound, usually a bit higher than home plate. Suppose he is pitching overhand. He lets go of the ball just above his head. The ball comes down just a bit

as it nears the plate. The faster it's thrown, the less it drops.

The pitch travels a nearly level path, but down just a bit. And that's the path you should swing your bat in—nearly level but up just a bit to meet the ball.

If you want to aim at something, aim to hit the ball right at the brim of the pitcher's cap. Don't worry, you're not likely to hit the pitcher, but there's a good chance that you'll hit a line drive somewhere.

What if the pitcher throws sidearm? The same thing—swing level with the pitch in the same path the pitch travels on the way to home plate.

Suppose you swing level, time your swing correctly, and connect. Will you hit a line drive?

Not all the time. Look at these bats.

If you hit the ball here, you'll probably hit a line drive.

If you hit the ball here, you'll probably hit the ball higher in the air for a fly ball.

And if you hit the ball here, you'll probably hit a ground ball.

27

But if you swing level and hit a grounder, it may often be fast and low to the ground. And if you hit a fly, it may often be deep to the outfield. So you'll have good chances on these balls too.

Try to hit line drives. Even if you don't get a line drive, you'll still have a better chance to get a base hit.

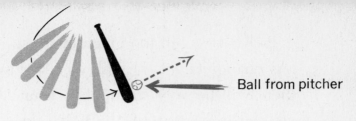

Ball from pitcher

What happens if you swing up too much? You'll hit more high flies.

And if you swing down, you'll tend to beat the ball into the ground.

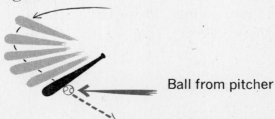

Ball from pitcher

29

Either way, up too much or down, you'll have less chance to hit the ball at all. Why? Because there will be only one spot in your swing where you can connect with the ball.

When you swing level with the pitch, there are many places in your swing where you can connect with the ball.

If you swing before the ball reaches the plate, you'll "pull" the ball.

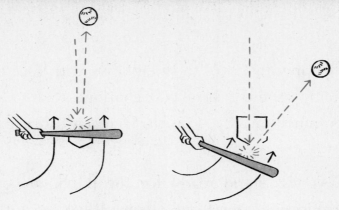

If you meet the ball when it's over the center of the plate, you'll hit it to center field.

And if you swing a bit late, you'll still be able to hit to the opposite field.

Suppose you try to swing level with the pitch, but for some reason you continue to hit down too much or up too much. Here's a tip that may help.

As you stand ready for the pitch, move the position of your front elbow. If you're a right-handed batter, your front elbow will be your left elbow. Raise your elbow just a bit. This will often make it easier to swing level.

Running the bases

In most baseball leagues for grade-school boys, you can't steal bases. You can't lead off from bases. And you can't run before the pitch reaches home plate. There are a couple of things, though, you can practice.

The first one sounds funny:
Run when you hit the ball.

You've probably seen it happen. The batter

hits the ball and then stands at home plate watching to see where it went. Finally, he runs. And often, he loses his chance to get a base hit or a safe trip to first base.

So run.

Run even if you think the ball is a foul. It could also be fair.

Run, even if you think it's an easy ball to catch. The fielder might drop it.

34

Run whenever your bat touches the ball. You'll find out on your way to first base whether it's a foul, an easy catch, a hit, or an error.

Foul line

Another good habit: *Run to first base outside the foul line.* If you run in fair territory and get hit by your own batted ball, you're out. Or, if you're in fair territory and interfere with a fielder making a play, you can be called out for interference. But you're always OK if you run to first base outside the foul line. And it's no farther to run.

The same is true when running from third base to home plate. Run just outside the foul line. Then you can't be called out for touching a batted ball or for interfering with the play of a fielder.

Very important: *Always run past first base.* Run hard, touch the bag, and keep on running

hard until you're past it. Don't slow up. You can't be tagged out beyond first base as long as you stay in foul territory. If first base is as far as you can get on the play, just trot back to the bag in foul territory and you're completely safe.

And if you do have a chance to run for second base, you can make a wide turn without losing speed.

tips on fielding

Your glove

Your glove is a good friend. It lets you catch hard-hit balls. Ground balls. Fly balls. Even when a ball is "too hot to handle," your glove is your shield. With it you can block the ball or knock it down.

41

When you're wearing your glove, there's no reason to be afraid of the ball, even when it's hit hard right at you. That's not always easy to learn, but when you do, you'll be a better fielder.

Your glove is not meant to catch the ball all by itself. Even the best fielders use both hands—their glove and bare hand.

When you catch a fly ball, your glove will be facing the ball. Your bare hand will be right next to it ready to capture it once it's in your glove.

And again, when you catch a ground ball, your glove will face the ball. And your bare hand will be ready to capture it once it's in your glove.

44

Handling ground balls

The first rule in handling ground balls is—get in front of the ball. Do this whether you're playing the infield or the outfield.

If the ball is hit wide to your left or to your right, you may not always be able to get in front of it. Maybe all you can do is get your glove on it. But most ground balls hit in your direction will give you time to move. Use that time to get squarely in the path of the ball.

The reason for this is simple. If you stand to one side and stick out your glove, there's lots of room above, below, and around your glove where the ball can get past.

Get in the path of the ball. Then there's not much room for the ball to get past you. You can knock it down or block it, at the very least. And the ball will be in front of you where you can grab it quickly and make the play.

Suppose the ball hits a stone or takes a bad bounce. If you're in front of it, you'll be able to jump either right or left to get it.

But if you're to one side, you'll have much less chance to catch it.

Once your body is squarely in the path of a ground ball, "charge it"—run up on it.

Imagine this play. The batter hits a bouncing ball in your direction and starts running to first base. You get in front of the ball, but wait for it to come to you. By the time you catch it and throw to first base, it may be too late to make the put-out.

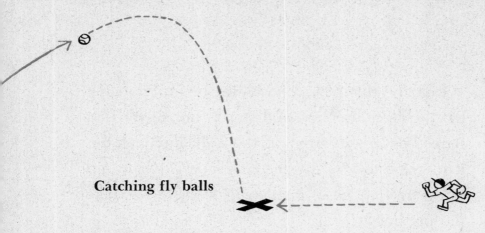

Catching fly balls

When a fly ball is hit to your position in the field, run as hard as you can to the spot where you think the ball will drop. Get there fast.

50

If the ball is hit hard or dropping fast, you may just get there as the ball does. But if it's a high fly, you'll often get there before the ball does.

Use that time to keep yourself in line with the ball. Place your body so that the ball is coming right to your chest.

51

Sometimes wind will change the path of the ball. Or maybe you didn't judge it exactly. Keep moving, changing your position, to keep in line with the ball until it's in your glove.

Why is it best to line up your chest with the ball? Because it centers you in the ball's path.

If you lined up the ball with your head, the fly might be farther than you thought, and go over your head.

And if you lined the ball up with your feet or knees, it might drop short.

Thinking a play ahead

This is a tough one, but it often makes the difference between a good player and an average one.

Let's look at an example. Imagine that you're playing shortstop. There's a runner on first base. Only one out. Now, before the pitcher throws the next ball you should have it clear in your mind what to do if the ball is hit to you.

A fast grounder? You could throw to second base for a force-out. And you might even get a double play.

A slow grounder? The runner at first has a good jump so the force-out at second is risky. But you can still throw to first for the put-out.

A line drive? You catch it for the out. But a quick throw to first would also get the runner off first for a double play.

When a play starts, things happen fast. You won't have time to decide what to do in all cases.

Thinking ahead on every play is hard. But practice it. Some people call it "having your head in the game." All the pros think ahead.

tips on pitching

Holding the ball

There are many ways to hold a baseball. Regular ways for common pitches. Special ways for tricky pitches.

But we're only going to show you one or two. Why? Because the first job of a pitcher is to throw the ball *hard, fast,* and *over the plate.* Learn to do this before thinking about curve balls, sliders, knucklers, and so forth. The fast ball is the only pitch you need worry about now.

How do you throw a fast ball?

One way is to grip the baseball with two fingers across the seams.

Or, you can grip the ball using two fingers along the seams.

And some pitchers like to use only one finger across the seams.

In each case, the ball is thrown straight, off the fingers. No twists. Use the way that gives you the most speed, and the best control.

When you pitch, throw hard and fast. See if you can really control your pitches. Get them in at the knees when you want to. Or high and outside when you want to. If you can do this, you won't have to worry much about the hitter's hitting, or walking either.

Most ball fields have a pitcher's mound, a small mound which puts the pitcher just a bit higher than the batter. This helps the pitcher. It makes it easier for him to throw hard.

In the middle of the mound is the pitcher's rubber. This also helps the pitcher. It gives him support for his back foot while he is throwing.

Some pitchers use a wind-up. Others do not. Do what is comfortable for you. But always have your back foot squarely against the rubber when you make your pitch.

If you wind up, you may not start with your foot against the rubber. But this is where it should be while you're throwing. This position gives you a firm feeling and adds power. And it lets you put your entire body into the pitch.

Learn to use your whole body when you pitch. You'll throw harder and better.

Pitching strikes

Should you throw full overhand, three-quarter overhand, or sidearm? Everyone is different. Which way feels the easiest, the most natural to you? Which can you control the best?

Whichever you decide, control of your pitches is worth thinking about. It takes plenty of practice. And even great pitchers have trouble with their control at times.

When you throw full overhand, it is probably easier to keep your pitches over the plate—between the inside and outside edges of the plate. But you may have trouble keeping the ball between the shoulders and the knees of the batter.

Here's a tip that may help. If your pitches are mostly too high, take a little longer stride off the mound as you throw. This will often bring your pitches down.

Or, if your pitches are mostly too low, take a little shorter stride off the mound as you throw. This will often bring your pitches up.

67

When you throw sidearm, it will probably be easier to keep your pitches between the shoulders and knees of the batter. But you may have trouble keeping your pitches over the plate.

Let's suppose you're a right-handed pitcher throwing to a right-handed batter. If your pitches to him keep going outside, move your stride a little bit more toward third base. This may help you pitch right over the plate.

Or, if your pitches are too far on the inside, move your stride a little bit toward first base.

What if you're a three-quarter overhand pitcher? You're in between the full overhand and sidearm delivery. You could have control problems in any direction.

When you do have control problems, try changing your stride off the mound when you throw. Just a bit longer or shorter for pitches that are too high or too low. Or, more toward third base or more toward first base for pitches that are too far outside or too far inside.

There's something else you can try, too. If you have trouble keeping the ball over the plate, pitch a little more overhand. This will give you better control.

Or, if your control problem is keeping the ball between the batter's knees and shoulders, pitch a little more sidearm.

When making these changes, do a little at a time. It doesn't take much to upset your control. It may not take much to get it back.

Think about these tips. And practice. Even big league stars practice so they can play better. They make mistakes (everybody does). But they learn from their mistakes and improve with practice and by playing the game. And so will you.